To Malcolm –
   Read wi[...]
your wonde[...]
Madison –

forever dad

forever dad

inspiring words on fatherhood

edited by sean keogh

Published in the United States in 2006
by Tangent Publications
an imprint of
Axis Publishing Limited
8c Accommodation Road
London NW11 8ED
www.axispublishing.co.uk

Creative Director: Siân Keogh
Editorial Director: Anne Yelland
Designer: Simon de Lotz
Production Manager: Jo Ryan
Production Controller: Cécile Lerbière

ISBN 1-904707-31-9

9 8 7 6 5 4 3 2 1

Printed and bound in China

about this book

This is a collection of wit and wisdom based on the theme of fatherhood. Written by and for dads and their children of all ages, it offers a witty, wry, and poignant look at what it means to be a father, how to face the challenges, revel in the delights, and generally pass on the wisdom of other fathers, sons, and daughters.

These remarkable thoughts and sayings are full of joy, anticipation, fulfilment, and goodwill. They have been drawn together from real dads and their families and friends. The sayings are complemented by a series of amusing animal photographs and are guaranteed to inspire.

This is an ideal gift book for fathers and fathers-to-be as a reminder of this special relationship.

about the author

Sean Keogh has worked in publishing for several years, on a variety of books and magazines covering a wide range of subjects. From the many hundreds of contributions that were sent to him by fathers and their children, from all over the world, he has selected those that best sum up what being a dad is all about.

Becoming a father's easy,
being a daddy is difficult.

To a father growing old, nothing is dearer than a daughter.

The only man a girl
can rely on is her dad.

Dad: a son's first hero,
a daughter's first love.

A dad is a person
who is loving and kind.

Any man can be a father
but it takes someone
special to be a dad.

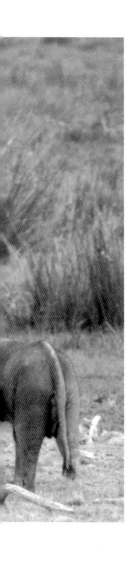

Every father should
remember that one day
his son will follow his
example, not his advice.

A dad is your biggest fan,
even when you strike out.

A father holds your
hand at the fair.

A father provides
for everyone.

The best inheritance you
can leave your kids is
a good example.

Good fathers
make good sons.

A father is worth more than a hundred schoolteachers.

Dad, your guiding hand
on my shoulder will remain
with me forever.

A father is a banker
provided by nature.

The greatest gift I ever
had came from God
and I call him dad.

Fathers are men who
give daughters away to other
men who aren't nearly good
enough so they can have
grandchildren who are
smarter than everybody else's.

Father is another
name for love.

The love of a father is one of nature's greatest masterpieces.

By the time you realize your father was right, you will probably have a son who thinks you are wrong.

You've got to do your own growing, no matter how tall your father was.

In any fathering situation
you have a 50 percent
chance of being right.

It is a great moment in life when a father sees his son grow taller than he or reaching farther.

Dads teach their kids
all about life…

…kids teach their dads
what life is all about.

A father doesn't tell you
how to live…

…he lives and lets you
watch him do it.

A truly rich man is
one whose children run
into his arms when his
hands are empty.

Dads turn frowns to smiles
in a split second.

A father is a man who expects
his children to be as good
as he intended to be.

Children are poor
men's riches.

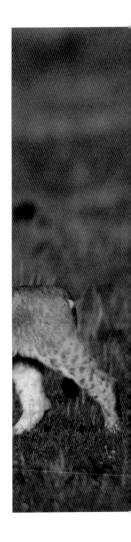

A good dad tells you
that you can be anything
you want.

There is perpetual summer
in a father's heart.

Dad lets you eat ice-cream
for breakfast…

…but only if mom isn't there.

Who my father was
doesn't matter…

…what I remember
about him does.

The greatest gift a father
can give his son is to
believe in him.

If you want your kids to be blameless, you have to be blameless yourself.

My father's hand expressed
kindness he could not
put into words.

I love to play hide and seek with my kid, but some days my goal is to find a hiding place where he can't find me until after high school.

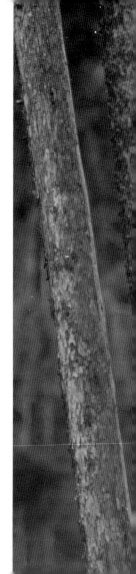

A father is a guiding light who shows you the way.

A father takes lots
of pictures but is
never in them.

A family without a father
is like a house
without a roof.

My father was the best and wisest person I ever knew.

You never outgrow your
need for your dad.

Education is something you get when your father sends you to college. But it isn't complete until you send your son there.

The greatest misfortune that can happen to an ordinary man is to have an extraordinary father.

What a father says to his children will not be heard by the world, but it will be heard by posterity.

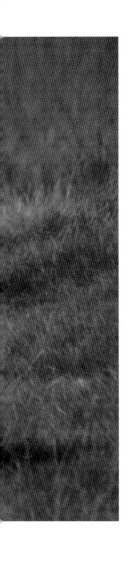

I didn't get to choose
my dad…

…fortunately my mom
had great taste.

A father is a guiding hand
who shows us the way.

The strongest need in childhood
is for a father's protection.

Fathers have a way of
putting things together.

A small boy becomes a big man thanks to his father.

All the qualities that
have helped me through
the hard times I got
from my father.

Anything which parents
have not learned from
experience they can now
learn from their children.

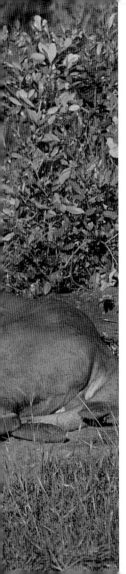

Being a father is the most
rewarding job of all.

Tell your children you
love them every day.